*SOCIETY:* an ensemble of individuals living in an organized group and sharing common interests.

Most animal species choose to live in a society. They gather in herds, shoals, colonies; they create flocks, packs, and swarms. What drives them to live together? How do they organize themselves? Throughout the Earth, even in its farthest ends, we find almost as many instances of kindred fellowship as there are species!

Joanna Rzezak

# ENSEMBLE

## animals in harmony

PETER PAUPER PRESS, INC.
White Plains, New York

To reduce the risk of
being devoured by
a large predator . . .

To help hide from predators, the backs of
herring are darker than their bellies. So, when
seen from below, herring don't stand out against
the luminous background of the sky. And when
seen from above, their dark backs serve as
camouflage against the marine background.

## . . . herring cluster together in SHOALS.*

In the Atlantic Ocean, shoals of herring include many thousands of fish! The greater their numbers, the less chance each one has of being caught. When a seal, a whale, or a shark attacks, it eats the first fish it finds in its path. So, all the fish are constantly trying to get to the center of the shoal to avoid being exposed.

And since everyone can't be in the center at the same time, their movement creates a gigantic whirlwind! The shoals form especially at night, when predators hunt. With the arrival of sunlight, the shoal disperses.

*Words followed by an asterisk are included in the glossary at the end of the book.

# To find love . . .

*A flamingo couple builds their nest in the mud and sand, where they lay an egg. Then, the mother and the father will each take turns covering the egg.*

... pink flamingos meander
in FLAMBOYANCES.*

These groups of magnificent birds move around freely in shallow waters along the sea coast, where couples appear discreetly. The partners feed each other. The distinctive shape of their beaks allows them to rummage through the mud, filtering it out to find food—small mollusks, crustaceans, and especially pigmented plankton, to which they owe the pink color of their feathers. Their long legs allow them to unearth their meal even in deep water. With their very supple necks—the longest of all birds—they sometimes form interesting shapes, including hearts!

Nothing escapes the
numerous watchful eyes . . .

. . . of hundreds of gnus gathered into HERDS.*

In the African savanna, these herbivores* find abundant food. But they are also
especially vulnerable there and must cooperate to spot potential predators.
Each individual in the herd keeps a close eye on the plain around them.
A threat is quickly detected!

Many animals would want to devour a gnu: lions, hyenas, leopards, cheetahs,
and even crocodiles. So the power of gnus is in their numbers. On occasion a large
herd of gnus can face a lion, confront it, and sometimes pursue it! A large herd
of gnus is made up of several harems.*

With their somewhat lopsided lines and curves, the poor gnus are often thought of as the ugliest animals in Africa.

Packing themselves tightly against each other to warm up . . .

. . . vipers form a
GENERATION.*

*Widespread throughout Europe, vipers are reptiles.
These animals are cold-blooded* and therefore need to
warm themselves, by taking advantage of the sun or
by gathering together in generations.*

One species of vipers among the most common in Europe, *Vipera aspis*, keeps their babies inside their bodies and only gives birth when the newborns are self-sufficient. The mother's body temperature has to be very high. So she warms herself in the sun and can form generations with other vipers in order to stay warm. Other snakes hibernate,* huddled against each other in generations to keep their bodies at the right temperature.

To survive in the forest and hunt together . . .

### ...wolves live in PACKS.*

In the Siberian taiga (boreal forest)—in Russia—wolves fight daily for survival. A pack of wolves is a family made up of two parents and their pups between the ages of one and three years old. Only the parents can reproduce; they are the ones who direct the pack, its hunt, and its movements. Everyone helps and protects one another in the pack. Gradually, the pups take on more and more duties. The most responsible will take care of the younger wolf pups. When they grow up, most wolves end up leaving the pack to find a mate and start their own family.

In order to move more calmly during periods of molting . . .

...a CAST* of spider crabs piles up in a pyramid on the seabed.

These gigantic crabs live in the Mediterranean Sea. As a spider crab matures, it outgrows its shell and has to change it. This shedding is called molting. By molting, the crab can grow and rid itself of certain parasites. This is a sensitive period, as its body is vulnerable because it loses its protection. The pyramid of crabs is difficult for predators—rays and sharks—to penetrate; thus, the young spider crabs find safe haven underneath the pyramid.

Certain migratory birds take advantage of air currents* to propel them so they can travel across greater distances using less effort.

. . . geese fly in GAGGLES* that
form the shape of a V.

If you've ever watched the Tour de France or any other bicycle race, you know that within the group the cyclists ride behind the leader of the race, to take advantage of his or her speed and therefore be less affected by wind resistance. With the arrival of autumn, geese, like many other birds, begin to migrate* from the north toward warmer climates in the south. Sometimes they fly thousands of miles! This voyage requires great effort and they have to prepare for it. And so, before their departure, they renew their feathers, accumulate a layer of fat, and develop their pectoral muscles. During the flight, geese, like cyclists, travel with a guide in the lead. The guide takes on the task of facing the wind and is regularly replaced. The spacing between geese in the group is important in order to have a clear view and avoid whirling spirals of air that form when the other geese beat their wings.

Well organized when it comes to taking care
of their little ones . . .

. . . COLONIES* of penguins
create nurseries where they
can leave their children.

Emperor penguins take care of their children communally. One or more adults keep watch over the daycare center while the others go fishing. All the little penguins gather together in a circle and huddle against each other with their heads bowed in order to stay warm. This formation is called "tortoise" because it resembles the military practice of Roman soldiers who assembled in this way to protect themselves with their shields. The habitat of emperor penguins is the Antarctic, the coldest place on Earth. These birds have developed bodies that resist the deep cold of their environment. Equipped with very thick plumage, feet that do not freeze, and a hardy layer of fat beneath their skin, they are very resistant. But penguins are especially astute in acting together to retain heat. The adults squeeze together, huddling against each other and changing places regularly so that the same ones are not always the most exposed to the cold on the circle's exterior.

Living together is not always convenient!
Sometimes you have to learn to share
food and space . . .

*Because of their great volume and bulky appearance, we tend to imagine that hippopotamuses are slow and lazy. Nothing is further from the truth: this is a highly aggressive animal that can easily become irritated and pursue its target very rapidly (from 18 to 25 mph/30 to 40 km/h) even outside the water. This is the most dangerous of all African animals.*

## ...Members of a BLOAT* of hippopotamuses often jostle each other in the water.

In Africa, hippopotamuses spend half their lives on land and the other half in rivers or lakes. With the coming of the dry season, the water begins to evaporate and the available space there—that is to say, the cool space of water—begins to diminish. Hippopotamuses, which don't withstand heat very well, huddle together to stay in the water. Because they are very individualistic despite their group living, they keep shoving and pushing each other! The lowering water level uncovers the large backs of these animals.

Certain birds take advantage of this. Hippopotamuses' bodies are covered in many types of algae and mushrooms—a feast for birds and a free cleaning for the hippopotamuses! A male reigns in the bloat. Those who do not wish to subject themselves to him, beware: they must either defeat the leader in battle or abandon the group. Misunderstandings can be frequent and sometimes deadly!

What a show in the skies! But why . . .

## ...do MURMURATIONS* of thousands of starlings fly in such ripples?

Ever more present in large cities, where they take advantage of the heat and abundant food, these hundreds of small birds stage magnificent shows for us. Their synchronized ballet fascinates scientists, who attempt to understand their logic. We now know that there is not a conductor in the group. Each bird can initiate a new movement, and its peers follow it, one after another.

By creating very dense flocks,* the murmuration protects the starlings from attacks from birds of prey, which will not venture into the midst of the crowd for fear of being injured. It is only latecomers and those separated from the group that are vulnerable. To sleep in safety, starlings gather together at night in the crowns of trees—amazing dormitories.

In a true model of female solidarity . . .

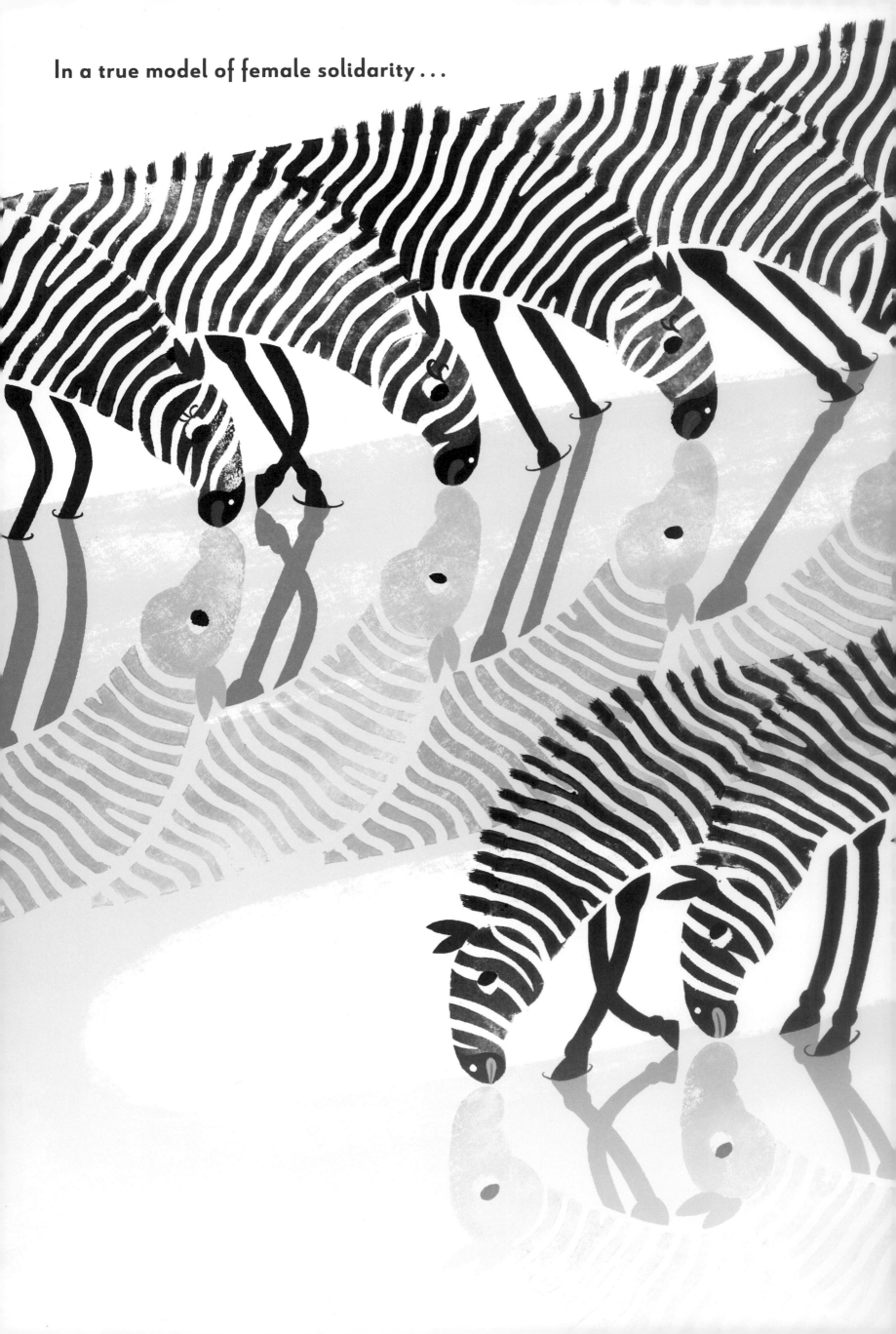

## ...female zebras form HAREMS.*

Harems of zebras wander the savanna. In each of these groups of females, there is a male—a stallion—who dominates. When this male becomes too old, he leaves the harem and joins a group of stallions. The mares—females—are very united and form very strong social connections. They also enjoy reciprocal grooming! A hierarchy forms within the harem. The dominant mare guides the group while the male stays in the back. A harem also monitors its surroundings to spot predators: lions, cheetahs, or leopards. The stripes on each zebra's body are different and probably allow them to be less visible to flies: they disrupt the vision of these insects, making it difficult for them to land on the zebra's body.

In order to find water and to take better care of babies . . .

*Adult males live alone. They only join herds to find a partner. They locate them thanks to the females' trumpet calls.*

## ...MEMORIES* of elephants move in family herds.

Elephants form matriarchal societies—power belongs to the females! Numerous adult females roam the savanna accompanied by their calves. The herd is guided by the oldest female elephant, called the matriarch. She has much experience and an excellent memory, giving her the ability to locate sources of water, which are so rare in their environment. During the dry season, thirst is constant. The herd follows the matriarch in their search for food and water.

To ensure the survival
of their offspring . . .

...Kemp's ridley sea turtles lay their eggs at the same time.

Some species of turtles, among which are Kemp's ridley sea turtles, practice synchronized egg-laying. Females get together by the hundreds during breeding season to lay their eggs on the same beach in Mexico. This mass birth is called *arribada* in Spanish, which means "arrival."

Each turtle burrows into the sand to lay an impressive number of eggs (sometimes hundreds of them!), compensating for those that crabs and vultures will snatch. Depending on the air temperature, the eggs will develop and become either males or females. Once they've left their shell, the babies try to reach the ocean as fast as possible without being devoured by predators. Then the babies let the sea currents carry them until they reach the age of three.

To share their daily tasks . . .

## ...baboons form a herd, sometimes called a TROOP.*

In a troop of baboons, political games are rampant: plots, hierarchies, and coalitions abound. A troop can consist of up to two hundred individuals. It is composed of numerous harems, each one having a dominant male and a few young submissive males.

Baboons are constantly moving, with marching orders in effect. The males go in front, followed by the females, while the young are relegated to the end of the group. Strict precautions are essential: in the savanna, danger can emerge at any moment!

# Traveling by the thousands is magical! . . .

By beating their wings up to
10 times per second, these butterflies
can travel nearly 621 miles (1000 km)
without stopping!

# ...A SWARM* of butterflies migrates in very large numbers.

Monarch butterflies gather together to migrate in succession toward the South, then the North of the American continent. These insects like to spend the winter in warm climates, in Mexico or in California. They have very fragile bodies that don't allow them to survive the negative temperatures of the North in winter. To prepare themselves for the long voyage, they spend the end of August nourishing themselves to create great energy reserves of fat (up to a third of their initial weight!). Once they arrive in warmer climates, the swarms rest on pine branches every night and sleep together in safety. Despite the miniscule weight of each individual, their accumulated mass bends the tree branches!

**Finally, doing things together is simply more fun!**

*Dolphins will favor the group at their own expense. There have been cases where several dolphins propped up a wounded friend at the water's surface so that the injured one could breathe.*

# Dolphins have known this for a long time and surf together in PODS!*

Being in a group isn't always about survival methods—sometimes it's just about the joy of being together! Dolphins adore surfing in the waves and often go to the coasts to practice their moves together. It's their way of playing and socializing!

# GLOSSARY

**Air current:** like sea currents, these are "corridors" in which air moves at a different speed

**Bloat:** a group of hippopotamuses

**Cast:** a collection of crabs grouped together

**Cold-blooded:** cold-blooded animals are those with an internal body temperature that varies according to the environment, as opposed to warm-blooded animals, which have a constant internal body temperature

**Colony:** gathering of animals that live together

**Flamboyance:** flock of flamingos

**Flock:** gathering of animals into a compact group

**Gaggle:** a group of geese

**Generation:** a pit or den of vipers, which group together in a nest

**Harem:** an ensemble of females defended by a single male

**Herbivore:** animal that eats only plants

**Herd:** large group of domestic or wild animals that live together

**Hibernate:** to spend the winter in a shelter or a temperate place

**Memory:** a herd of elephants

**Migrate:** to move to another environment

**Murmuration:** a flock of starlings

**Pack:** a group of animals, often referring to dogs or wolves, that live and/or hunt together

**Pod:** a colony of dolphins

**Shoal of fish:** large quantity of fish gathered together

**Swarm:** group of insects that fly together

**Troop:** gathering, collection; a herd of baboons